STEN F

POEM

For Elizabeth, with love and thanks, T.M.

JANETTA OTTER-BARRY BOOKS

Come Into This Poem copyright © Frances Lincoln Limited 2011
Text copyright © Tony Mitton 2011
Illustrations copyright © Caroline Holden 2011

First published in Great Britain in 2011 by
Frances Lincoln Children's Books, 4 Torriano Mews,
Torriano Avenue, London NW5 2RZ
www.franceslincoln.com

A catalogue record for this book is available from the British Library.

ISBN: 978-1-84780-169-2

Illustrated with frottage and line drawings

Set in AromaLT and StantonICG

Printed in the United Kingdom by CPI Bookmarque, Croydon in June 2011

1 3 5 7 9 8 6 4 2

COME iNTO THiS POEM

Poems by
TONY MITTON

Illustrations by
CAROLINE HOLDEN

F

FRANCES LINCOLN
CHILDREN'S BOOKS

Contents

Garden

The door is open
to the garden.

It is a box
of life

where sunlight pulls
green magic
from brown earth.

Sit, and you will see
how breezes shake the leaves,
scattering shadows,

as insects spin their chances
on the air.

Big Red Boots

Big red boots, big red boots.
One of them squeaks and the other one toots.
One of them hops and the other one stamps.
Big red boots take long, wet tramps.

Boots, boots, big red boots.
One of them squeaks and the other one toots.

Big red boots on busy little feet
start out shiny, clean and neat.
Big red boots, oh, yes, yes, yes,
end up muddy in a terrible mess.

Boots, boots, big red boots.
One of them squeaks and the other one toots.

Boots, boots, big red boots,
squelch through mud and trample roots.
Big red boots say, "Look! Oh gosh!
What a great puddle there... Yay! SPLOSH!"

Entrance

Come into this poem.
Step through this little gap
between the words,
and who knows what you'll find?
Some secret passage
tucked inside your mind?
A flight of steps
that wind
            down to a door
that opens on a wood
where once you stopped and stood?

Then through the trees
you think you hear a stream.
It whispers faintly
of a distant dream
in which you knelt
and looked into a pool
and saw your own face gazing,
clear and cool. . .

You stumble on
to find a lisping brook
whose ripples are
the writing in a book.
Its text is strange
and hard to understand.
And as the pages
flutter in your hand,
you snap it shut
to place it on the shelf...
then see you're in
the poem of yourself.

Invisible Ink

What do you do
with invisible ink?

Scribble your secrets,
the things that you think.
For the words disappear,
yes, they go with a p-l-i-n-k!

That's what you do
with invisible ink.

But I once heard the case
of a very sad guy –
I suppose that he worked
as some sort of a spy –
He wrote out a message
in curious code,
and he wrote in the blood
of a poisonous toad.
(It was dead when he found it,
right there on the road.)
It was squashed by a car,
and was starting to stink.

But its blood made a perfect
invisible ink!

He wrote down the words
and they all disappeared.
But listen to this,
for the next bit is weird.
Why he should try it
I really can't think. . .
He decided to drink
the invisible ink!

Ink, ink, invisible ink,
is something you never,
not ever, should drink!

To begin with he took
just the tiniest sip.
It glistened a bit
on his trembling lip.
Then he took a deep breath,
with a gulp and a frown,
lifted the bottle
and drank it all down!

Ink, ink, invisible ink,
it's OK for writing
the things that you think,
especially secrets
that make you turn pink.
But please say you'll never,
no, not as a dare,
not even in moments
so crazy and rare,
no, not under water
or up in the air,
no, not in the country
or here in the town,
not with a smile,
or a leer or a frown...
say that you'll never,
you'll not even think
to venture a drink
of invisible ink.

Cos, what of the spy?
He was gone in a blink!

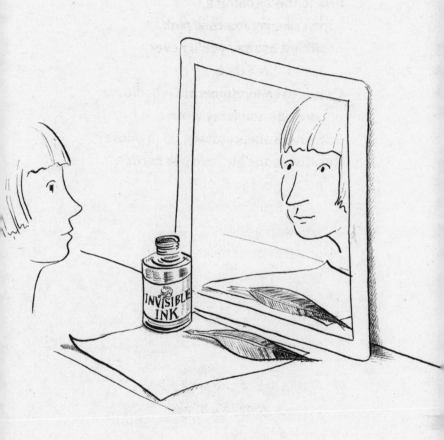

Cold Comfort Pets

My pets are in the garden.
I want them roaming free.
I don't like creatures in my lap
or sitting on my knee.

Ooh, look! There goes my woodlouse,
my beetle... and my worm!
But what's this climbing up my nose?
Aaaatchoooo! My own pet germ.

Death and the Knight

The knight rode home from the weary wars
at the end of his long crusade.
For two long years he had torn at the Turk
with his lance and his strong, broad blade.

But now that his banner hung tattered,
a rag on the listless breeze,
he was home to his lands and his castle
for some peace and some well-earned ease.

As he rounded a bend in the roadway
a raven flew up from the wood.
And there by the edge of the forest
a sinister figure was stood.

The figure was clothed in a long black robe
and his face showed solemn and pale.
As the knight drew level to meet with his gaze
his spirits began to fail.

Something about this figure
had a strangely familiar style.
Was it the frame, so long and so lean?
Or the twist of the thin-lipped smile?

"Good day to you, sir," the knight spoke up.
"I feel I have met you before.
But where it could be is a puzzle to me,
for I've long been away at the war."

The lean man spoke and his words blew as dry
as the dust where it drifts on the ground.
And it made the knight long for his lands and his home,
for his fire and his faithful hound.

"For two long years I have watched," came the words,
"as into each battle you'd ride.
For two long years I have gathered the souls
of the slain as they fell by your side.

But now that I stand by this bend in the road
it is you I am waiting to meet."
"First tell," cried the knight, "if it's death I must taste,
will my ending be bitter or sweet?

And what of my children, and what of my wife,
and what of my home and my lands?"
But Death only lifted his hourglass
with its pitiful, trickling sands.

"Could you not tarry an hour or two
till I catch just a glimpse of my home?"
But Death only caught at his bridle.
And all that he uttered was, "Come..."

And he led the knight into the dark of the wood
where the trees seemed to wrap them around.
Then the road to the castle lay empty
and the breeze stirred the dust on the ground.

• •

In the middle ages death was often represented as a figure, wearing
a long, hooded cloak and carrying a scythe and an hourglass. When it
was time for you to die, it was imagined that Death came in this form
to lead you away. The scythe stood for the cutting down of life, like
grass, and the hourglass represented the sands of time trickling away.

Magic Ride

Who can say how a carpet flies?
Perhaps by wishes, dreams and lies?

How does a carpet leave the ground?
By magic touch or secret sound?

How can a carpet ride the breeze,
with tassels tickling tops of trees?

Is there a way to understand
its airy flight above the land,

and how we see it hover, pause,
before it swiftly swoops and soars?

And should we trust it? Do we dare
its fabled flight through storied air?

Can there be some way to know
where it will land us, where we'll go,

whether we'll end up better, worse,
with blessing, or with bitter curse,

whether to let that carpet lie,
or take its trip across the sky?

Is there a way to help decide
whether to risk that magic ride?

Stay at home? Or dare depart?
The answer's written in your heart.

Dark

When light is bright
where does dark hide?

Inside a sack.
Down in each crack.
Shadowy, mischievous,
secretive, black.

Tucked in a corner.
Under a lid.
Rolled in the fold
of a cloth it lies hid.

Down in the cellar,
up in the loft,
dark waits so patiently,
silent and soft.

Inside your slipper
or deep in your pocket,
dark settles waiting
for night to unlock it.

It's inside the cupboard,
it's under the bed.
Just close up your eyes
and it's inside your head.

At the flick of a switch,
at the death of a flame,
what lies a-waiting,
oh, what is its name?

At the pull of a blind,
at the blink of a spark,
what fills the emptiness?
Yes, it's the dark!

There's nothing below it,
there's nothing above it.
It won't go away
so I'm learning to love it.

For, surely the dark
should hold nothing to fear,
as it's deep in the throat
and it's down in the ear.

And dark has a quality
soothing and deep:
it holds you and folds you
and lulls you to sleep.

But what does its velvety
voice sound like? Hark!
Nothing but silence
is spoken by dark.

It's what you emerge from,
the place before birth.
And it waits to receive
as they spade on the earth.

Is it an enemy?
Is it a friend?
Dark, ever faithful,
is there at the end.

Fantasy Cottage

Fantasy Cottage
is clean and bright.
Its roof is green
and its walls are white.

The doors and windows
are pink and neat.
It stands at the end
of Seaside Street.

Fantasy Cottage
is sweet and small.
The cobbles nestle
against its wall.

Look from the window,
step from the door,
out to the sky
and the pebbled shore.

Wonder

A little red bug on a leaf of green.
What is it for, what does it mean?

A small seed sprouting under the earth.
What is its purpose, what is it worth?

A ripening apple held in my hand.
What's in a fruit to understand?

Winter and summer, night and day.
Why do they turn, what do they say?

Restless planet under me,
full of life and mystery.

Hope

Sitting in my bath
I simply hope
that somehow I might catch
that slippy soap...

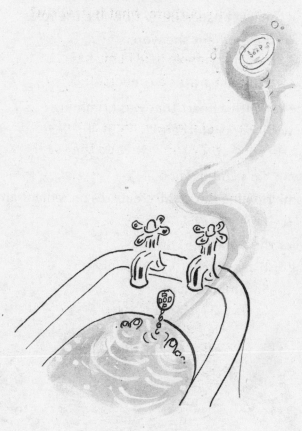

Kwan Yin

Kwan Yin sat quietly,
settling herself on a rock by the hard sea shore.

Kwan Yin breathed softly,
and the waves seemed to flow like the folds
    of the garment she wore.

Down by the waters
she sat with a heart that was brimming
    with mercy and care.

Kwan Yin's compassion
came rippling out to all creatures on radiant air:

Over the ocean,
the fish and the heron, the squid,
    the insomniac shark,

Over the daylight,
beyond the horizon, to soften the gathering dark,

Over the land,
where the ox and the farmer went ploughing
    with regular feet,

Over the mountain,
where solitary sages sat brooding in silent retreat,

Over the cities,
where princes and beggars were born to their high
    and low station,

Over the world,
with its curious customs and cultures, from nation
    to nation,

Up to the heavens,
where planets and comets and stars shone
    like silver above,

Kwan Yin sat quietly,
steadily giving her care and compassionate love.

∙ ∙

Kwan Yin (Ku'an Yin) is the Chinese *bodhisattva* (a kind of god
or goddess) of compassionate love and kindness. In paintings and
sculpture he/she is often shown sitting on a rock on the shore of
a legendary island home. It is never clear whether Kwan Yin is male
or female, though some say she embodies the best virtues of both.

Penny Piece

Sun up high,
sky so blue,
went for a walk,
nothing to do.

Branches sighing,
birds a-twitter,
down in the grass
saw something glitter.

Picked it up:
a simple penny,
nothing special,
one like many.

Kept it with me
all the same,
went on careless
till I came

upon a lake
that lay in trance,
threw my penny,
watched it dance,

spin and flicker
through the air,
down to meet
the water, where

sleeping surface
gasped awake
as that penny
hit the lake,

sending out
a circling shiver,
ripples racing,
liquid quiver,

till at last
the glassy pane
slept in silence
once again.

Lake asleep
and penny gone,
made a wish
and then walked on.

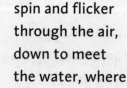
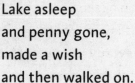

Dunwich, the Lost City

All gone under,
they have all gone under the sea,
the streets and the alleys, the stalls and the houses,
all of their glamour and glee.
All of the people, their brawls and their banter,
all of their frolic and fight.
All gone under,
swept from the land
by the sea, in the night.
And all of the churches,
their chants and their candles,
their hallowing incense and prayer,
swept from the world by undreamable forces
of water, of air.

Buttress and spire in a glorious soaring,
a marvel of masonry.
All gone under,
they have all gone under the sea.

And all of the jostle and bristle of business,
what, of such wealth, to remain?
Only a woodland, a crumbling clifftop, some rubble,
the wisp of a lane.

Only a remnant of wall and of churchyard,
a scatter of thicket and tree.

The rest has gone under.
It has all gone under the sea.

. . . .

In the Middle Ages Dunwich was one of the main ports of England
and an important centre of culture and religion. But one night,
in a terrible storm, most of it collapsed into the sea, leaving just a few
remnants on the cliff edge. It is said that on some nights when the sea
is rough you can just hear the bells in the steeples beneath the waves,
tolling mournfully for this old, lost city.

Teaser

What kind of ants
tear down trees?

What kind of ants
roll in mud
to take their ease?

What kind of ants
have four knees?

What kind of ants
flap their ears
in the breeze?

What kind of ants
spell their name
with two 'e's?

Ssh! Don't tell.
It's a tease.

Answer on p.92

Spring Sunshine

Drenching the pavement,
warming the wall,
bathing the cat
in a slumbering sprawl.

Shining the shell
on a beetle's back.
Feeding the weed
that springs from a crack.

Waking the buds
that break from the tree.
Shaking out gold,
and all for free.

Tale

The track I tread is hard and long.
And now my heart beats not so strong.

The day has dwindled to an end,
but, as I turn the trail bend,

I see a cottage in a glade,
a gentle dwelling couched in shade.

The door lies open as to say,
You're welcome here, come what may.

And by the step the air is sweet.
I take the boots from off my feet.

The room seems filled with quiet hours,
and lightly trimmed with simple flowers.

And in the corner stands a bed,
its pillow waiting for my head.

The bed is clean and freshly made,
a pallet where one's life is laid.

I peel the cover with a sigh,
and there upon the bed I lie.

Its fold is kind and warm, and deep.
And I can sleep. And I can sleep.

Txt PoM

Wht wll peple
thnk v nxt?
PoMs cmpsd
in mble txt!

Ltst thng
4m th hmn rce:
txt tht flots
in cbr spce.

Cmpct lttrs
on th scrn.
Wht do thA say?
Wht do thA mEn?

Rd thm thru
n snd rply.
Sht thm srng
thru th sky.

Whn Uve dne
+ als cmplte
scrl thm thru
+ prs dlte.

Text Poem

(Translation)

What will people
think of next?
Poems composed
in mobile text!

Latest thing
from the human race:
text that floats
in cyber space.

Compact letters
on the screen.
What do they say?
What do they mean?

Read them through
and send reply.
Shoot them soaring
through the sky.

When you've done
and all's complete,
scroll them through
and press delete.

Thunderbird

(the song of Little-Nose, the totem-carver)

I have sought the Thunderbird.
I have sailed far from home.
I have voyaged over the swell
and the wild sea-foam.

I have heard the Thunderbird
as each wide mighty flap
of its wings ripped the air
with the thunderclap.

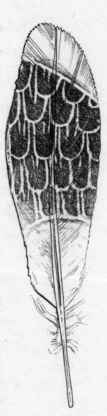

I have seen the Thunderbird.
I have watched it rise.
I have witnessed the lightning
lance from its eyes.

I have awed at the Thunderbird
hunting up high.
I have gasped as it lifted
a whale to the sky.

I have fronted its face
and its terrible beak.
I have told it my purpose
and heard it speak.

I have ridden its flight.
I have clung to its feathers
as it soared through the clouds
to scatter the weathers.

I have come back to tell
in the place of my birth
how the Thunderbird waters
our Mother Earth.

I have carved the Thunderbird
for all folk to see
up at the top
of the Totem Tree.

. . . .

The Thunderbird was a vast bird that controlled the weathers
for the natives of the north-west coast of America.
When the boy Little-Nose asked to become a carver, the adult
carvers told him in jest that he could only join them if he
carved an image of the Thunderbird (which no person had
ever seen in the flesh). Undaunted, Little-Nose set out in his
frail canoe and found this great spirit of the weathers. In return
for accepting Little-Nose's visit, and for flying him back to his
people, the Thunderbird demanded that his image be placed
at the top of all Totems. Little-Nose was the first to carve it.
(North-American Legend).

The Sandwich

I think I'll make a sandwich.
I'd better start with bread.
And then I'll put some butter on
or maybe marge instead.

I'll slap a slice of cheese in
and then a hunk of ham,
a little bit of chicken breast
and how about some jam?

Some sardines in a sandwich
are often rather nice –
and look! Here, in my larder,
I see some savoury rice.

A sandwich, to be healthy,
should hold some salad too.
And it seems a shame to waste this little
blob of Irish Stew.

I'm sure there's something missing.
I wonder what it is. . .
Ah, yes! Of course, some ketchup!
Kersplotch! Now, that's the biz!

But let me think... don't rush me.
I see no need to hurry.
This sandwich needs a little bit
of last night's mushroom curry.

I'm getting there, don't fuss me!
You nearly had me flustered.
I almost snatched that carton up
and squelched a layer of custard!

At last the job's completed.
But wait... I wonder whether
these strings of cold spaghetti
wouldn't hold it all together?

This sandwich is delicious,
if difficult to chew.
I'll never get through all of it.
Won't you have some too?

The Taper

The poet sat reading, alone in his hut,
by the light of a flickering taper.

The shadows played gracefully, stretching
    their shapes
on the luminous face of the paper.

Then in from the darkness came flying
    and flapping
a flittery creature of night.

It circled the flame of the taper, entranced
by the dangerous dance of the light.

The poet's attention was torn from his page
as the creature flew into the fire.

And he sat for a moment and thought
   on the strangeness
of dangerous thrill and desire.

'I would sit here reading,'
said the poet,
'by the taper's flickering light.

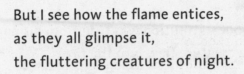

But I see how the flame entices,
as they all glimpse it,
the fluttering creatures of night.

And I see how they suffer,
frantically flapping,
as fire bites into their wings,

Until I can no longer relish,
for all of its virtues,
the knowledge my bright light brings.

And so I shall blow out the taper,
and then with moist fingers
I'll snuff out its dwindling spark,

To sit in the silence,
enlightened, and reading
the ponderous book of the dark.'

. . . .

This is an old Japanese tale which tells of a hermit poet.
When he saw how fatally attracted the moths and
insects were to the flame of his reading taper, he put it
out and sat in the dark to spare their lives.

Pigeon

Here comes pigeon,
peck, peck, peck,
fluffing his feathers
and puffing his neck,
strutting up and down
with a croon and a coo,
proud old pigeon,
how do you do?

Jazz River

The sure stream of the saxophone
goes pouring through,
meanders like a river,
strong and blue
              and softly flowing.

The slow glide of the saxophone
slides like a snake,
winding its way,
letting its course take
              a serpent passage.

Sweet horn blow smoothly,
for those blue notes
flow truly like a stream,

a swelling drift of sound
that winds along.

Jazz River, take us with you
on your journey.
Pull us with the current
of your song.

Three Ships

Three ships came sailing over the sea.
And what did they carry, oh what did they bear?
One brought a cargo of billowing air,
and who would have thought that a vessel so fair
could bring such a cargo to me?

Three ships came sailing over the sea.
And what did they carry, oh what did they hold?
One brought a cargo of light like gold,
and who would have thought that a vessel so bold
could bring such a cargo to me?

Three ships came sailing over the sea.
And what did they carry, oh what did they store?
One brought a cargo of wonder and awe,
and who would have thought that a vessel so braw
could bring such a cargo to me?

Three ships came sailing into my bay.
And what did they carry, oh what did they bring?
A cargo of love and of lyric to sing,
a cargo of poetry fit for a king,
a cargo of rhymes and of rhythms to swing.
And I sang as they swung in my bay.

The Ghost Horse

I saw the ghost horse through the trees
on a late midsummer night.
It cropped the grass in a forest glade
by a full moon's milky light.

Its breath was like a silvery haze.
It shambled through the dew.
Its phantom body seemed to shine
against the night's dark blue.

What horse was this? And from what place?
And why should it be there?
What eerie force had shaped it?
Was it of flesh or air?

I watched the horse transfixed, entranced.
I stood as still as stone.
Why should it graze mysteriously,
so quietly and alone?

And as I watched I heard a sound
that chilled me where I stood.
The strangest cry came echoing high
across the midnight wood.

The ghost horse rose its spectral head
in answer to the sound.
It shook its mane and stirred its hoofs
and stamped the leafy ground.

It disappeared into the wood,
between the stark, black trees.
And all it left was just a mist
that lingered on the breeze.

But as I turned and walked away
I heard a horn, and soon,
I saw the horse way up above,
against the silver moon.

The rider seated on its back
was but a gaunt, dark shape,
behind whose shoulders billowed out
a long and flowing cape.

I never saw that sight again,
but when the moon is high,
I sometimes fancy that I hear
the eerie midnight cry.

The Tea Song

After Charles Causley's "I Love My Darling Tractor".

I love my little teapot.
I love its pretty spout.
I love to see the steaming tea
come gently gliding out.

I love my cup and saucer.
I love the way they clink.
I love the way they seem to say,
"Sit down and take a drink."

I love my china tea-set,
the pot, the jug, the cup,
which, in the morning, when I'm yawning,
help to wake me up.

I love my dear old caddy
of scratched and dented tin.
Beneath its lid lies safely hid
the tea that I've put in.

I love my little tea-set,
so neat upon its tray...
Let's brew, right here, a piping cheer
for tea: *Sip, sip, hooray!*

Ponderous Frog

Ponderous frog,
by the water you squat,
sometimes blinking,
sometimes not.
What are you thinking?
Tell me. What?

Sometimes you're still,
sometimes you hop,
sometimes abscond
to the pond with a plop.

But frog, are you simple,
or are you wise?
Or merely intent
on catching flies?

You sit like a buddha.
You wait like a sage.
I never did witness
a frog in a rage.

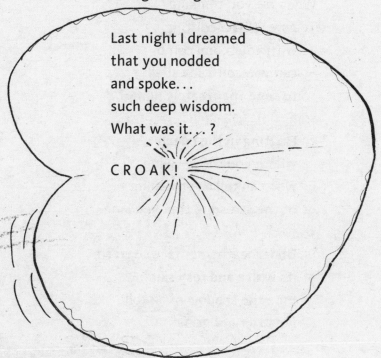

Last night I dreamed
that you nodded
and spoke. . .
such deep wisdom.
What was it. . . ?

C R O A K !

Mermaid

Mermaid in the waters,
gazing in your glass,
what is it you see there
as the proud ships pass?

As you sit a-coiffing
with your coral comb,
can you coil a sea-spell
to send them safely home?

Floating in the ocean
where you softly swing,
who can tell the meaning
of the sea-song that you sing?

Underneath your face so fresh,
its white and rosy skin,
I see the shadow of a skull,
I read a rigid grin.

Upon your breast there hangs a string
of shells that shine so fair.
For every shell I count a soul
that slumbers in your lair.

Mermaid basking on the waves,
though still I draw my breath,
I fear your twining arms will take me
dreaming to my death.

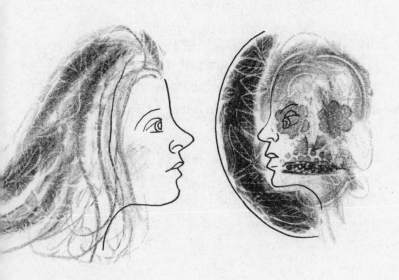

The White Horse of Uffington

They say there's a dragon high up on a hill.
She's not gone away, for she's running there still.
With the rain in her nostrils, the wind in her mane,
she gallops The Ridgeway again and again.

There's some that will have it the dragon's a horse,
but none who can tell why she canters her course.
And whether a steed of the earth or the air,
high up on the hill she goes galloping fair.

She races her way through the reaches of night,
as under the moon she goes glistening white.
And when the world's throbbing with skylark and sun
she covers the crest of the hill at a run.

The dragon is slender and supple and strong.
She straddles the hill as she gallops along.
The dragon is nimble and lissom as light.
Her spirit is wild and her body is bright.

The dragon's an arrow unleashed from a bow.
She whistles above and she plummets below.
She soars like a lance as it severs the air.
Then into the earth she goes quivering there.

The dragon's alive and the dragon's abroad.
She's sleek and she's silver and sharp as a sword.
And whether you give her your mind or your eye,
she'll gallop the earth and she'll soar through the sky.

They say there's a dragon high up on a hill.
She's not gone away, for she's running there still.
For ever and ever she'll canter her course.
So it's up and away for the Uffington Horse.

· ·

The White Horse of Uffington is cut into the chalk hillside below
Uffington Castle, an Iron Age Celtic hill-fort just off The Ridgeway
in Berkshire. The stylised design of the horse has been likened to one
seen on Celtic coins of the same period. It could be a sacred horse, an
animal holy to the Celts. But some people say it is a dragon. Just below
it is Dragon Hill, where St George is said to have slain his dragon. Whether
we choose to see it as dragon or horse, the figure has a wonderful energy
about it. It seems to be flying along, a beast both of air and earth. To me
it comes across as a powerful image of life-energy, carved into the loins
of the landscape.

The Fire Steeds

Have you seen the horses in the flames?
These are their names:
Goldmane, Flicker, Blue, Prance,
a herd of lungers and strivers
jostling in a strange dance,
a race to nowhere.

Did you see them gallop through the fire?
Higher and higher they went,
hellbent to get to heaven.
And, sure, by now,
in the grey hour
of morning ash and embers,
they will be there,
with fire all spent.
And in some pale, cool, watery meadow
they crop softly at damp grass,
nudging their hoofs through dew.
Their world is drenched.
Their thoughts are rippled blue
and green.
Their fire has been.
The flames are quenched.

Seed Spell

Bury me dark, bury me deep.
Let me lie awhile, asleep.

Let my root stretch out, uncoil,
sifting nurture from the soil.

Let me push my small shoot where
it reaches up to light and air.

Leaves uncrinkle, one by one,
soaking up bright rays of sun,

so that soil and light and air
help me grow at last to bear

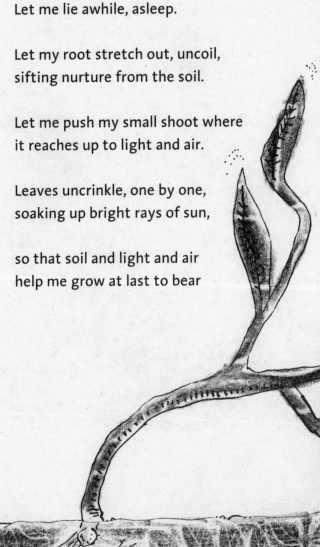

a flower that draws the fumbling bee
to store gold pollen at his knee...

and so the flower becomes a fruit
that holds a seed that grows a shoot

which, helped by soil and sun and rain,
begins the cycle once again,

as life goes slowly round and round
on Nature's strange, amazing ground.

The Blind Fiddler

Blind Fiddler, Blind Fiddler,
what tune is it you play?
Can it be a jolly jig
to dance my feet away?

Is it a rolling ballad
or an old, sad song
to pull upon my tender heart,
to make me wish and long?

Could it be a bold march
to stir my heart and head,
to make me yearn for courage
and a soldier's coat of red?

Or is it a lament
in a fine, keening plain,
a music of the moor
and the mist and the rain?

Blind Fiddler, when the moon is up
I fancy I hear float
the gently whispering ghost
of a fiddler's faint note.

But if I bend to listen
with a straining, eager ear,
it is nothing but the song
of a soft wind I hear.

Blind Fiddler, how fixed you stand,
ancient and alone,
listening to the secret music
locked within your stone.

. . . .

The Blind Fiddler is a standing stone, 3.3 metres (10 feet 9 inches)
tall, that can be seen near Catchall, Cornwall. Local legend says
The Blind Fiddler was turned to stone for making music on
the Sabbath Day (Sunday).

A keening plain is a wailing lament, a shrill mourning-song.

Shingle Street

Down at the end of Shingle Street
is a place where the waves and the shoreline meet.
It's there you can stand and bathe your feet,
down at the end of Shingle Street.

Out at the mouth of Briney Bay
is a place where the waters swing and sway.
You can rock in your boat and dream all day,
out at the mouth of Briney Bay.

Up at the top of Haven Hill
is a place where the air rests calm and still.
You can sit for hours and breathe your fill,
up at the top of Haven Hill.

Just at the edge of Waving Wood
is a place where the world grows green and good.
It's there that things can be understood,
just at the edge of Waving Wood.

Deep in the core of Hopeful Heart
is a place you can find a space apart.
It's here that a wish may sprout and start,
deep in the core of Hopeful Heart.

So pick up your spirits and stir your feet.
There's a shore to tread and a sea to greet.
Can you hear your heart as it starts to beat?
Come for a stroll down Shingle Street.

There really is a Shingle Street, on the coast of Suffolk, England.
It was there I got the idea for this poem. The other places, of course,
I made up.

Bat

Little mouse with leathern wings,
inaudible, so high it sings.

A twilight swoop, a dusky flitter,
a shadow-glimpse, a hint of twitter.

In barn or tower, or loft in town,
you'll find it hanging upside down.

Cahoots with owl and crone and cat,
a swirly, looping, spooking. . . bat.

Itchy Titchy

Some people keep enormous pets,
like goats or great big dogs.
While others go for smaller pets,
say, tortoises or frogs.

But mine's a very little pet,
a teeny, tiny titch.
I got it free – a frisky flea!
Eeeeouch! It's made me itch...!

The Salt Boy

I am the boy from underwave.
My home is in the deep.
But now you've brought me to the shore
I'll hide myself and weep.

I cannot live upon the land.
The air is dry and thin,
the ground too firm beneath my feet,
the harsh light hurts my skin.

I long to be beneath the waves
where waters wrap me round.
I long to lie within their lap,
lulled by their muffled sound.

The sea, she is my mother.
I love her steady sway.
She cradles me with languid arms
and rocks me in her bay.

I am the boy the netman caught.
He cannot feel my pain.
I pray he'll row me in his boat
and put me back again.

• •

A Celtic folk tale tells of a boy brought out of the sea by
a fisherman. The boy had gills and was clearly distressed to find
himself on land. The fisherman wanted to show him at fairs,
but the local priest ordered him to put the boy back in the sea
where he belonged.

Web

Nothing could be stranger
than the beauty and the danger
of your shiny silver net.

Nothing quite so tangly
as the web so sleek and dangly
that your needle legs can knit.

Nothing quite so cunning
as the spin that you set running
from your sticky spider spit.

Nothing quite so gruesome
as the struggling bugs so juicesome
that your tricky trap can get.

Small Church, Sleeping

Within the circle
of its sacred wall
I glimpsed the chapel
dappled with the sun.

It sat upon its tump,
so safe, secure,
surrounded by the graves
of old and gone.

And just beyond its wall
the passing traffic
went pressing on the hill,
both up and down.

But in this little space
of dappled quiet
the light and shade, the stone
dreamed on and on.

Will o' the Wisp

A will o' the wisp will guide you
over the marsh by night.
A will o' the wisp will lead you on
with its will o' the wispish light.
A will o' the wisp will take you
through a tangle of bush and briar.
A will o' the wisp will tease you
with its will o' the wispish fire.
A will o' the wisp is wicked,
so mischievous, merry and mean.
Yes, a will o' the wisp is a bit of a wit
you'll wish you had never seen.
For a will o' the wisp will show you the way
and you'll follow in faith, but then
you'll trip on a log and you'll slip in a bog
and you'll never be seen again.

• •

Some people say that a will o' the wisp is just marsh gas, an eerie
but natural phenomenon that occurs on moors and marshes. But
some still hold that it is a wilful and wanton being that delights
in leading lost travellers to their doom.

Worm

I'm a little wiggler.
I'm a little worm.
Watch me as I wriggle.
See me as I squirm.
Find me in the garden
sliding through the earth.
Go and ask the gardeners.
They know what I'm worth.

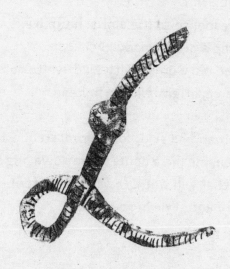

Glengorm, The Blue Glen

The gentleman looked at his fine, new house
where it stood so proud and high.
He saw how it lorded it there in the glen
with its towers that touched the sky.

And he thought to himself, "I must give it a name,
a name that will suit it well,
a name that suggests its beauty and power
to all who can talk and tell."

As if in response to the words he spoke,
he noticed a peasant pass by,
a wizened old woman with wild, white hair
and a fierce, bright glint in her eye.

"Old woman," he said, "one word, I request.
Will you name me a name for my dwelling?
A name that will suit it, a name to describe
its nature and style in the telling?"

The old woman eyed him directly
and smiled as she spoke to him then.
"Glengorm," she uttered, "would suit it.
For Glengorm holds the meaning 'Blue Glen'."

The gentleman gazed at the hue of the sea
and the islands so shadowy blue.
"Glengorm," he murmured, and thought how the name
seemed suitable, beautiful, true.

He turned to give thanks to the woman
but she seemed to have passed on her way.
So Glengorm was the name that he gave to his house.
Glengorm it was called from that day.

But to all of the people who lived in those parts
the 'blue' was not wistful or soft.
The 'blue' was the smoke that had filled up the glen
as the factors set fire to each croft.

Yes, the blue had been bitter and acrid
as it rose from their thatches aflame.
And the way they were turned from their livings
was ever held fast in that name.

Glengorm, Blue Glen, The Glen of the Smoke,
was the meaning the woman had thought.
And there in a word was recorded
how dearly that fine house was bought.

The Glengorm in question is on the Isle of Mull in the Hebrides
off the west coast of Scotland. The poem records a local legend which
tells how the fine house there got its name.

The "factors" is the name given to the men who were employed by
landlords to clear the crofters out of their crofts. This process has come
to be called "The Clearances". Whole communties in some parts were
put out of their homes. Their thatches were fired to discourage them
from returning to their crofts once they had been turned out and
moved on. This is a bitter episode in Scottish history.

Shell Villanelle

I am a snail. This shell is where I hide.
The world is full of danger, threat and spite.
My brittle canopy feels safe inside.

My way is slow. A snail's pace I slide.
I have no speed, no means of sudden flight.
I am a snail. This shell is where I hide.

With steady caution through the world I glide.
If shadows loom, or things flash fast and bright,
my brittle canopy feels safe inside.

I cannot parry stabbing beaks with pride,
nor wear my armour like a valiant knight.
I am a snail. This shell is where I hide.

If jabbing birds should come, all glitter-eyed,
I have no way to stand at bay and fight.
My brittle canopy feels safe inside.

But for this case, I'd long ago have died.
And so this spell I steadily recite:
I am a snail. This shell is where I hide.
My brittle canopy feels safe inside.

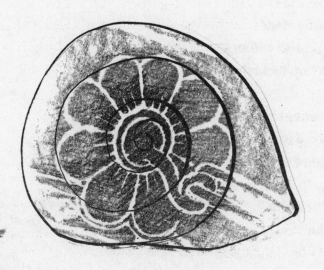

The Villanelle is a poetic form. It follows a set structure.
Villa is the Latin word for 'house'.

Yarn (The Writer's Tale)

Do you remember
the tale of the girl
locked up in the chamber,
and told to spin gold
from straw?

I am like her.
My world is a vault
of solid stuff,
brutal and tough,
and I am locked up in it.

My wheel is my pen
and my work is to set it
to spin,
to grip with its small point
all it can pin
down.

Was it a witch
or a king,
who spelled me here,
pitching me into
this pent place?

Why should I ask,
as clearly my task
is merely to write
and write and write,
across the desert
of day and night,

endlessly spinning
the dead, dry straw
into a glimmer
of something more,

plying my pen
to subtly fold
the lustreless straw
to a sheen of gold?

My story is over.
The tale is told.

Days

Old day, gold day,
where did you go?

Over the skyline,
sinking low.
Into the arms
of the waiting night
to nestle myself
in its dark delight.

New day, blue day,
what will you bring?

Light in the sky
and a song to sing.
Sun bobs brightly
up with the dawn,
spreading warmth
as the day is born.

91

Answer to Teaser (page 38)
elephants
(Note: the elephant is the only animal
that has 4 knees, truly)

© Kate MacRae

Tony Mitton has been reading and writing poems since he was 9, and began writing specifically for children around the age of 40. He used to work as a primary school teacher and special needs teacher but now focuses full time on his writing. He performs his work in schools, libraries and book festivals across the UK. His first book of poems for Frances Lincoln was *Plum*.
Tony lives in Cambridge with his wife. They have two children, now in their twenties.

www.tonymitton.co.uk

MORE POETRY FROM
FRANCES LINCOLN CHILDREN'S BOOKS

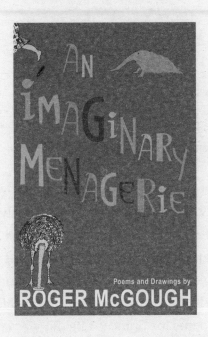

978-1-84780-166-1 • PB • £5.99

An A-Z of animal poems with a difference!
Choose your favourite from Roger McGough's
witty and wicked menagerie.

"Classic Roger McGough" – *Guardian*

978-1-84780-167-8 • PB • £5.99

With wordplay and riddles, and poems that will make
you laugh, tell you stories and make you think, this is
a brilliant debut from an exciting new poet.

"A box of delights" – *Carol Ann Duffy*

978-1-84780-168-5 • PB • £5.99

Perfect for younger children, these poems are fresh,
funny and brilliant for reading aloud.

"These poems are born out of years of visiting
infant classrooms. A real birthday party of words" –
Pie Corbett